W9-BBY-611

HEALTHY COOKING

LOW CHOLESTEROL

CLB 2435
© 1991 Colour Library Books Ltd, Godalming, Surrey, England
All rights reserved
This edition published in 1991 by Gallery Books,
an imprint of W.H. Smith Publishers, Inc.,
112 Madison Avenue, New York 10016
Printed and bound in Singapore
ISBN 0 8317 8046 0

Gallery Books are available for bulk purchase for sales promotions
and premium use. For details write or telephone
the Manager of Special Sales, W.H. Smith Publishers, Inc.,
112 Madison Avenue, New York, New York 10016 (212) 532-6600.

GALLERY BOOKS

FOR YOUR HEART'S SAKE

Introduction

Health and diet are inextricably linked to such a degree that none of us can afford to regard healthy eating simply as a fad. Heart disease in particular, is one of the most common fatal conditions in the Western world, and one of the most crucial factors which causes this is a high cholesterol diet.

Cholesterol is a fatty substance found in all animal tissue and it is also produced in the body by the liver. Essentially, cholesterol is needed to carry fats through the bloodstream. Problems occur when too much fat builds up and is left on the walls of arteries, narrowing them and restricting the blood flow around the body. If this flow becomes completely blocked, a heart attack will occur.

In order to reduce excess cholesterol we must change our eating habits by reducing the amount of animal tissue and animal fat which we eat.

Research has shown that by eating non-animal fats the blood levels of cholesterol can actually be reduced. The reason being that vegetable fats are mainly polyunsaturated and these help to regulate the blood flow and keep the arteries clear of fatty deposits. Polyunsaturated fats from vegetables can therefore be included freely in a low cholesterol diet but high fat animal products such as red meat, pork and dairy foods must be restricted. Fish contains a type of fat called mono-unsaturated, which has no effect on cholesterol levels and can therefore be included in your diet without any detrimental effect. Shellfish, however, are very high in cholesterol and should be avoided completely.

One point to watch out for is that some products, such as margarines, are not always as "healthy" as their packaging suggests. A production method called hydrogenation actually changes polyunsaturated fats into saturates, so look on labels and do not buy items which contain "hydrogenated vegetable oils" or "hydrogenated unsaturated fats."

These low cholesterol recipes have been developed to offer a wide choice of favorite items which combine healthy eating with flavor and variety. So delve inside and you will realize that as well as protecting your health, nutritious food can also tickle your taste buds.

SERVES 4-6

ONION SOUP

This delicious recipe demonstrates that food which is good for your heart need be neither bland nor boring.

¼ cup polyunsaturated margarine
2lbs onions, peeled and thinly sliced
3 tsps sugar
½ cup all-purpose flour
7½ cups chicken stock or water
Salt and freshly ground black pepper
1½ tsps dried thyme
½ cup dry white wine or dry sherry
12 x 1-inch slices French bread
3 tbsps olive oil
½ cup grated Cheddar cheese, optional
Fresh parsley for garnish

Step 1 Brown the onions in a large saucepan with the margarine and sugar.

1. Melt the margarine in a large saucepan. Stir in the onions and add the sugar. Cook uncovered over a low heat, stirring occasionally, for 15-20 minutes or until the onions become golden brown.

2. Stir the flour into the onions and cook for 1 minute.

3. Gradually pour the stock into the onions, mixing well with each addition to blend smoothly.

4. Season with the salt, pepper and thyme, and add the wine or sherry. Return the soup to a low heat and bring to the boil.

5. Partially cover the saucepan, then simmer the soup for 20-30 minutes.

6. Brush each side of the slices of bread lightly with the olive oil and arrange them on a metal rack in a broiler pan.

7. Lightly toast one side of the bread under a hot broiler until it turns pale gold.

Step 6 Lightly brush the slices of bread with the olive oil.

8. Turn the slices of bread over and sprinkle with the grated cheese, if used.

9. Return the slices of bread to the broiler and cook until the cheese has melted and is golden brown, or if the cheese is not being used, until the other side of the bread has been lightly toasted.

10. Serve the soup in individual bowls with 2 or 3 of the croutons floating on the top. Garnish with fresh parsley.

Cook's Notes

Time
Preparation takes about 20 minutes, cooking takes about 45 minutes-1 hour.

Freezing
This soup freezes very well, but the croutons should be prepared fresh each time.

Cook's Tip
The addition of sugar will help the onion to brown. For a paler soup, omit the sugar and gently fry the onions until they are just soft and not browned.

Fat Type
Chicken stock contains fairly small amounts of saturated fat. The cheese contains a higher amount, but is used in such small quantities that this should not matter. Use vegetable stock and omit the cheese if desired.

SERVES 4

CELERY AND APPLE SOUP

This interesting combination of flavors produces a tasty soup that is also suitable for vegetarians.

2 tbsps polyunsaturated margarine
1 large onion, peeled and finely chopped
3 cooking apples, peeled, cored and sliced
5 cups vegetable stock
1 bay leaf
Salt and freshly ground black pepper
3 sticks of celery, finely chopped
Finely sliced celery for garnish

Step 2 Gently cook the apples with the onion until it begins to soften.

1. Melt the margarine in a large pan and stir in the onions. Fry gently for 5 minutes, or until the onions are soft but not browned.

2. Add the apple to the onion mixture and cook for a further 3 minutes, or until the apple begins to soften.

3. Stir half the stock into the onion and apple, along with the bay leaf and seasoning. Bring the mixture to the boil, cover and simmer for half an hour. Remove the bay leaf.

4. Put the remaining stock into another pan along with the celery. Bring to the boil, then cover and simmer for 30 minutes.

5. Using a liquidizer or food processor, blend the onion and apple mixture until it is smooth.

6. Beat the puréed onion and apple mixture into the pan containing the stock and celery.

7. Return the pan to the heat and bring back to the boil. Garnish with the celery sticks and serve immediately

Step 4 Cook the celery in half of the stock, simmering until it is tender.

Step 6 Beat the puréed onion and apples into the stock and celery, mixing well to blend evenly.

Cook's Notes

Time
Preparation takes about 15 minutes, cooking takes about 45 minutes.

Serving Idea
Serve with whole-wheat rolls or a French stick.

Freezing
This recipe freezes well.

Fat Type
This recipe contains no saturated fat at all.

SERVES 6

MINESTRONE SOUP

There are numerous different recipes for minestrone. This one is high in fiber, which helps to reduce cholesterol levels in the blood, and it has hardly any saturated fats at all.

½ cup dried white cannellini beans
5 cups vegetable stock
3 tbsps olive oil
1 large onion, peeled and finely chopped
1 clove garlic, minced
1 stick celery, thinly sliced
2 carrots, peeled and diced
¼lb spring greens, finely shredded
½ cup cut green beans
1 large zucchini, trimmed and diced
¼lb tomatoes, peeled, seeded and diced
1 bay leaf
⅓ cup whole-wheat pasta
1½ tbsps fresh chopped basil
1½ tbsps fresh chopped parsley
Salt and freshly ground black pepper

1. Put the beans into a large bowl and cover with the vegetable stock. Leave to soak overnight. During this time the beans will double in volume.

2. Heat the oil in a large saucepan and gently fry the onion and garlic until they have softened, but not browned.

3. Stir in the celery, carrots, spring greens, green beans and zucchini. Fry gently, stirring until they have just began to soften.

4. Add the beans with the stock to the pan of vegetables, along with the tomatoes, bay leaf, pasta and seasoning. Bring to the boil, then cover and simmer for about 1 hour, or until the beans are very tender. Stir occasionally during this time to prevent the ingredients from sticking.

5. Stir in the basil and parsley, heat through for 5 minutes and serve immediately.

Step 1 Soak the beans overnight in the vegetable stock. They will double in volume during this time.

Step 4 Add the beans and stock to the partially cooked vegetables.

Cook's Notes

Time
Preparation takes about 20 minutes, plus overnight soaking for the beans. Cooking takes about 1½ hours.

Serving Idea
Serve with crusty whole-wheat rolls.

Watchpoint
It is most important to cook any dried beans very thoroughly as they can be dangerous if eaten before they are sufficiently cooked.

Variation
Use red kidney beans instead of the white cannellini beans in this recipe.

Fat Type
Olive oil contains polyunsaturated fat and the pasta contains negligible amounts of saturated fat.

SERVES 4

VICHYSSOISE

Although this French soup is usually eaten cold, it also delicious served hot.

3 large leeks
2 tbsps polyunsaturated margarine
1 medium-sized onion, peeled and sliced
2 medium-sized potatoes, peeled and thinly sliced
2½ cups vegetable stock
Salt and ground white pepper
1¼ cups skim milk
Finely chopped parsley or chives, for garnish

1. Trim the top and bottom from the leeks and peel away the outer leaf.

2. Slit the leeks lengthwise down one side cutting right into the center of the vegetable.

3. Hold the leek under running cold water, allowing it to wash any bits of soil or grit from in between the leaves.

4. Slice the leeks very thinly using a sharp knife.

5. Melt the margarine in a saucepan and add the leek and sliced onion. Cover and allow to sweat gently over a low heat for about 10 minutes.

6. Add the potatoes to the leek mixture, and pour in the stock.

7. Season with the salt and pepper, cover and cook gently for 15 minutes, or until the potatoes are soft.

8. Using a liquidizer or food processor, purée the soup until it is smooth.

9. Return the puréed soup to the saucepan and stir in the milk. Adjust the seasoning and reheat very gently until it is almost boiling. Remove from heat.

10. Either serve the soup immediately or allow to cool, then chill in a refrigerator for at least 2 hours.

Step 2 Slit the leeks lengthwise down one side, cutting into the center of each vegetable.

Step 3 Hold the slit leeks under cold running water, allowing it to penetrate between the leaves to wash out any soil or grit.

Step 8 Purée the leek and potato mixture in a liquidizer or food processor, until it is very smooth.

11. Serve garnished with the finely chopped parsley or chives.

Cook's Notes

Time
Preparation takes about 15 minutes, plus chilling time. Cooking takes about 30 minutes.

Serving Idea
Serve with lightly toasted slices of whole-wheat bread.

Freezing
This soup freezes very well.

Fat Type
This soup contains a minimal amount of saturated fat in the milk.

SERVES 4

CHICKEN SATAY

This typical Indonesian dish is very spicy, but uses ingredients which are all low in fat, making it an excellent appetizer for four.

3 tbsps soy sauce
3 tbsps sesame oil
3 tbsps lime juice
1½ tsps ground cumin
1½ tsps turmeric powder
3 tsps ground coriander
1lb chicken breast, cut into 1-inch cubes
3 tbsps peanut oil
1 small onion, very finely chopped or minced
1½ tsps chili powder
½ cup crunchy peanut butter
1½ tsps brown sugar
Lime wedges and coriander leaves, for garnish

1. Put the soy sauce, sesame oil, lime juice, cumin, turmeric and coriander into a large bowl and mix well.

2. Add the cubed chicken to the soy sauce marinade and stir well to coat the meat evenly.

3. Cover with plastic wrap or a damp cloth and allow to stand in a refrigerator for at least 1 hour, but preferably overnight.

4. Drain the meat, reserving the marinade.

5. Thread the meat onto 4 large or 8 small skewers and set aside.

6. Heat the peanut oil in a small saucepan and add the onion and chili powder. Cook gently until the onion is slightly softened.

7. Stir the reserved marinade into the oil and onion mixture, along with the peanut butter and brown sugar. Heat gently, stirring constantly, until all the ingredients are well blended.

Step 5 Thread the marinated meat onto 4 large, or 8 small, kebab skewers.

Step 9 Brush the partially broiled chicken with a little of the peanut sauce to baste.

8. If the sauce is too thick, stir in 2-4 tbsps boiling water.

9. Arrange the skewers of meat on a broiler pan and cook under a preheated moderate broiler for 10-15 minutes. After the first 5 minutes of cooking, brush the skewered meat with a little of the peanut sauce to baste.

10. During the cooking time turn the meat frequently to cook it on all sides and prevent it browning.

11. Serve the skewered meat garnished with the lime and coriander leaves, and the remaining sauce separately.

Cook's Notes

 Time
Preparation takes about 25 minutes, cooking takes about 15 minutes.

 Serving Idea
Serve with a mixed salad.

 Variation
Use a selection of fresh vegetables instead of the chicken to make a vegetarian alternative, which would contain no saturated fat at all.

 Fat Type
Chicken contains low amounts of saturated fat. The remaining ingredients contain unsaturated fats.

SERVES 4-6

SPICY VEGETABLE FRITTERS WITH TOMATO SAUCE

This delicious dish makes a ideal appetizer or interesting snack. Use any favorite vegetables or those that are in season.

1 cup all-purpose flour
1 cup whole-wheat flour
1½ tsps salt
1 tsp chili powder
1½ tsps ground cumin
1¼ cups water
1½ tbsps lemon juice
1 small cauliflower, broken into small flowerets
1 eggplant, cut into 1-inch cubes
3 zucchini, trimmed and cut into 1-inch pieces
2 cups button mushrooms
1 red pepper, seeded and cut into ¼-inch thick rounds
1 green pepper, seeded and cut into ¼-inch thick rounds
1 large potato, peeled and cut into 1-inch cubes
1⅔ cups canned plum tomatoes, drained
1 red chili, seeded and chopped
1 clove garlic, minced
1 small onion, peeled and finely chopped
1½ tbsps white wine vinegar
1½ tbsps soft brown sugar
Salt the freshly ground black pepper, to taste
1 sliced green chili for garnish
1 sliced red chili for garnish

1. Put the flours, salt, chili powder and cumin into a large bowl. Make a slight well in the center.

2. Gradually add the water and lemon juice to the flour, beating well until a smooth batter is formed.

3. Wash the fresh vegetables and allow them to drain completely on paper towels or a clean cloth.

4. Put the tomatoes, fresh chili, garlic, onions, vinegar and sugar into a food processor or liquidizer and blend until the sauce is smooth.

5. Pour the sauce mixture into a small pan and heat gently, stirring until it is completely warmed through. Season with salt and transfer to a small serving dish and garnish with slices of red and green chilies.

6. Heat some vegetable oil in a deep fat fryer until it is warm enough to brown a 1-inch cube of bread in just under 1 minute.

7. Make sure the vegetables are completely dry, patting any moisture off them with paper towels if necessary.

8. Using a slotted spoon drop the vegetables, a few at a time, into the batter and dip them to coat thoroughly.

9. Remove the vegetables from the batter, again using the slotted spoon, and allow some of the batter to drain back into the bowl.

10. Drop the vegetables into the hot oil, and fry quickly until they are golden brown and the batter puffy.

11. Remove the fried vegetables from the oil and drain completely on paper towels, keeping them warm until all the remaining vegetables have been prepared in this manner.

12. Serve immediately, providing small forks with which to dip the vegetables into the spicy tomato sauce.

Cook's Notes

Time
Preparation takes about 20 minutes, cooking takes about ½ hour.

Watchpoint
It is important to ensure that the vegetables are completely dry before coating with the batter, or it will not cover them.

Fat Type
There is no saturated fat in this dish, but it is important to check that the oil used in the deep fat frying is polyunsaturated and that it is fresh.

SERVES 6

TUNA, BEAN AND TOMATO SALAD

Fish is of great value in a low cholesterol diet as it contains mono-unsaturated fats which do not affect the cholesterol level in the blood.

1 cup dried flageolet beans
6oz canned tuna in brine
Juice of 1 lemon
⅔ cup olive oil
1½ tsps chopped fresh herbs, e.g. parsley, basil or marjoram
Salt and freshly ground black pepper
8 firm tomatoes

1. Put the beans into a bowl and pour over enough cold water to just cover. Allow to soak overnight.

2. Drain the beans and put them into a saucepan. Cover with boiling water, then simmer for at least 1 hour. Drain thoroughly and cool.

3. Drain the can of tuna and flake it into a bowl.

4. Put the lemon juice, olive oil, herbs and seasoning into a small bowl and beat together with a fork.

5. Stir the beans into the tuna fish and mix in the dressing, tossing the salad together carefully so that the tuna does not break up too much, but the dressing is thoroughly incorporated.

6. Adjust the seasoning and arrange the salad in a mound on a shallow serving dish.

7. Cut a small cross into the skins of the tomato and plunge them into boiling water for 30 seconds.

8. Using a sharp knife carefully peel away the skins from the tomatoes.

9. Slice the tomatoes thinly and arrange them around the edge of the bean and tuna salad. Serve immediately.

Step 5 Mix the dressing into the salad by tossing it carefully, to ensure that the tuna does not break up too much.

Step 8 When blanched, the skins on the tomatoes should peel away very easily if you use a sharp knife.

Cook's Notes

 Time
Preparation takes about 25 minutes, plus overnight soaking.

 Variation
Use any type of bean of your choice.

 Watchpoint
Great care must be taken with cooking beans, as any that are under cooked could be dangerous when eaten.

 Fat Type
This recipe contains mono-unsaturated and polyunsaturated fats.

 Serving Idea
Serve with a simple lettuce salad.

SERVES 4

SMOKED MACKEREL PÂTÉ

Smoked fish has a wonderful flavor and is ideal for making pâté.

8oz smoked mackerel fillets, skin and bones removed
¼ cup polyunsaturated margarine
Juice of half an orange
1½ tsps tomato paste
1½ tsps white wine vinegar
Salt and freshly ground black pepper, optional
1 x 3½ oz can pimento peppers, drained
1¼ cups clear vegetable stock
3 tsps powdered gelatin
3 tbsps dry sherry
3 tbsps cold water

1. Put the mackerel, margarine, orange juice, paste, vinegar and seasonings into a liquidizer or food processor and blend until smooth.

2. Put the pâté into a serving dish and smooth the top evenly.

3. Cut the pimentos into thin strips and arrange in a lattice over the top of the pâté.

4. Bring the stock to the boil in a small pan. Remove from the heat and cool for 1 minute.

5. Sprinkle over the gelatin and allow to stand, stirring occasionally until it has completely dissolved.

6. When the gelatin has dissolved the liquid should be

Step 3 Arrange the strips of pimento in a lattice pattern over the top of the pâté.

Step 5 Sprinkle the gelatine over the hot stock and allow it to stand, to dissolve completely.

clear. At this point stir in the sherry and cold water.

7. Very carefully spoon the aspic over the top of the mackerel pâté and the pimentos, taking great care not to dislodge the lattice pattern.

8. Chill the pâté in a refrigerator until the aspic has completely set.

Cook's Notes

 Time
Preparation takes about 30 minutes, plus chilling time.
Cooking takes about 2 minutes.

 Variation
Use any type of smoked fish in place of the mackerel in this recipe.

 **Preparation**
If you do not have a food processor or blender, this pâté can be made by mashing with a fork, but it will not have such a smooth texture.

 Fat Type
Fish contains mono-unsaturated fat which does not affect the cholesterol level in the blood.

 Serving Idea
Serve with crusty whole-wheat bread or French toast.

SERVES 4-6

TOMATO AND PEPPER ICE

Similar to frozen gazpacho, this appetizer is ideal for serving on warm summer days. It could also be used, in smaller quantities, as a palate freshener between courses in place of a conventional sweet sorbet.

6 ice cubes
½ cup canned tomato juice
Juice 1 lemon
1½ tsps Worcestershire sauce
½ small green pepper, seeded and roughly chopped
½ small red pepper, seeded and roughly chopped

1. Break the ice into small pieces using a small hammer.

2. Put the broken ice into a blender or food processor, along with the tomato juice, lemon juice and Worcestershire sauce. Blend the mixture until it becomes slushy.

3. Pour the tomato mixture into ice trays and freeze for ½ hour, or until it is just half frozen.

4. Using a sharp knife, chop the peppers into very small pieces.

5. Remove the tomato ice from the freezer trays and put it into a bowl.

6. Mash the tomato ice with the back of a fork until the crystals are well broken up.

7. Mix in the chopped peppers and return the tomato ice to the freezer trays.

8. Re-freeze for a further 1½ hours, stirring occasionally to prevent the mixture from solidifying completely.

9. To serve, allow the tomato ice to defrost for about 5 minutes, then mash with the back of a fork to roughly break up the ice crystals. Serve in small glass dishes which have been chilled beforehand.

Step 2 Blend the ice, tomato juice, lemon juice and Worcestershire sauce until it becomes a smooth slush.

Step 6 Mash the semi-frozen tomato ice with the back of a fork to break up the ice crystals finely.

Step 8 During the freezing time, keep stirring the tomato and pepper ice with a fork, to prevent the mixture from becoming a solid block.

Cook's Notes

 Time
Preparation takes about 15 minutes, plus freezing time.

 Freezing
This recipe will freeze for up to 2 months.

 Watchpoint
Take care not to allow the tomato ice to freeze into a solid block, or it will be too hard to break into rough crystals.

 Serving Idea
Scoop out the tomatoes and serve this ice in the shells, instead of glass dishes.

 Fat Type
There is no fat in this recipe.

SERVES 4

SUMMER PASTA SALAD

Lightly cooked summer vegetables and whole-wheat pasta are combined to create this delicious wholesome salad.

1 eggplant
1 zucchini
1 red pepper
1 green pepper
1 medium-sized onion
2 large tomatoes
6 tbsps olive oil
1 clove garlic, minced
Salt and freshly ground black pepper
1⅓ cups whole-wheat pasta spirals
1½ tbsps vinegar
¾ tsp dry English mustard

Step 1 Sprinkle the eggplant slices liberally with salt and allow them to de-gorge for 30 minutes to remove their bitterness.

1. Cut the eggplant into ½-inch slices. Sprinkle the slices liberally with salt and allow to stand for 30 minutes.

2. Using a sharp knife, trim the zucchini and cut into ¼-inch slices.

3. Cut the peppers in half and carefully remove the cores and seeds. Using a sharp knife, cut the pepper into thin strips.

4. Peel and finely chop the onion.

5. Cut a small cross in the skins of the tomatoes and plunge them into boiling water for 30 seconds. After this time remove the tomatoes and carefully peel away the skins.

6. Cut the peeled tomatoes into 8. Remove and discard the pips from each tomato slice.

7. Put 3 tbsps of the olive oil in a frying pan and stir in the onion. Fry gently until it is transparent, but not colored.

8. Thoroughly rinse the salt from the eggplant slices and pat them dry on absorbent paper towels. Roughly chop the slices.

9. Add the chopped eggplant, zucchini, peppers, tomatoes and garlic to the cooked onion and fry very

Step 9 Gently fry all the vegetables together, stirring frequently to prevent them from browning.

gently for 20 minutes, or until just soft. Season with salt and pepper and allow to cool.

10. Put the pasta spirals in a large saucepan and cover with boiling water. Sprinkle in a little salt and simmer for 10 minutes or until tender but still firm.

11. Rinse the pasta in cold water and drain very well.

12. Beat together the remaining olive oil, the vinegar and mustard in a small bowl. Season with salt and pepper.

13. Put the pasta and cooled vegetables into a serving dish and pour over the dressing, tossing the ingredients together to coat them evenly. Serve well chilled.

Cook's Notes

Time
Preparation takes approximately 40 minutes, cooking takes 30 minutes.

Preparation
Make sure that the eggplant is rinsed very thoroughly or the salad will be much too salty.

Fat Type
Olive oil contains polyunsaturated fat and is therefore beneficial to those on a low cholesterol diet.

SERVES 4

MUSHROOM PASTA SALAD

Mushrooms are always delicious in a salad and this recipe, which combines them with whole-wheat pasta shapes, is no exception.

7½ tbsps olive oil
Juice of 2 lemons
1½ tsps fresh chopped basil
1½ tsps fresh chopped parsley
Salt and freshly ground black pepper
2 cups mushrooms
1⅓ cups whole-wheat pasta shapes of your choice

Step 1 Beat the lemon juice, herbs and seasoning together in a large bowl using a fork.

1. In a large bowl mix together the olive oil, lemon juice, herbs and seasoning.

2. Finely slice the mushrooms and add these to the lemon dressing in the bowl, stirring well to coat the mushrooms evenly.

3. Cover the bowl with plastic wrap and allow to stand in a cool place for at least 1 hour.

4. Put the pasta into a large saucepan and cover with boiling water. Season with a little salt and simmer for 10 minutes, or until just tender.

5. Rinse the pasta in cold water and drain well.

6. Add the pasta to the marinated mushrooms and lemon dressing, mixing well to coat evenly.

7. Adjust the seasoning if necessary, then chill well before serving.

Step 2 Use a sharp knife to slice the mushrooms thinly.

Step 6 Stir the cooled pasta into the marinated mushrooms, mixing well to coat evenly.

Cook's Notes

Time
Preparation takes approximately 10 minutes, plus 1 hour at least for the mushrooms to marinate. Cooking takes about 15 minutes.

Variation
Use a mixture of button and wild mushrooms for a delicious variation in flavor.

Serving Idea
Serve mushroom pasta salad on a bed of mixed lettuce.

Fat Type
Olive oil contains polyunsaturated fat and is beneficial for those on a low cholesterol diet.

SERVES 4-6

STIR-FRY TOFU SALAD

Ideal for vegetarians, but so delicious that it will be enjoyed by everyone.

1 cake of tofu
¼lb snow peas
½ cup mushrooms
2 carrots, peeled
2 sticks celery
½ cup broccoli flowerets
⅔ cup vegetable oil
4½ tbsps lemon juice
3 tsps honey
1½ tsps grated fresh ginger
4½ tbsps soy sauce
Dash of sesame oil
4 green onions
½ cup unsalted roasted peanuts
1 cup bean sprouts
½ head Chinese cabbage

1. Drain the tofu well and press gently to remove any excess moisture. Cut into ½-inch cubes.

2. Trim the tops and tails from the snow peas.

3. Thinly slice the mushrooms with a sharp knife.

4. Cut the carrots and celery into thin slices, angling your knife so that each slice is cut on the diagonal.

5. Trim the green onions and slice them in the same way as the carrots and celery.

6. Heat 3 tbsps of the vegetable oil in a wok or large frying pan. Stir in the snow peas, mushrooms, celery, carrots and broccoli, and cook for 2 minutes, stirring constantly.

7. Remove the vegetables from the wok and set them aside to cool.

8. Put the remaining oil into a small bowl and beat in the lemon juice, honey, ginger, soy sauce and sesame oil.

9. Stir the sliced green onions, peanuts and bean sprouts into the cooled vegetables.

10. Mix the dressing into the salad vegetables, then add the tofu. Toss the tofu into the salad very carefully so that it does not break up.

11. Shred the Chinese cabbage and arrange them on a serving platter. Pile the salad ingredients over the top and serve well chilled.

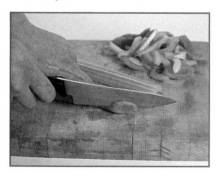

Step 4 Slice the carrots and celery thinly, cutting with your knife at an angle to produce diagonal pieces

Step 10 Toss the tofu very carefully into the salad ingredients taking care not the break it up.

Cook's Notes

Time
Preparation takes approximately 25 minutes, cooking takes 2-4 minutes.

Preparation
Make sure that the stir-fried vegetables are completely cool before adding the remaining salad ingredients, or they will lose their crispness.

Variation
Shredded cooked chicken can be used in place of the tofu in this recipe.

Fat Type
All the fat in this recipe is polyunsaturated.

SERVES 6-8

MIXED PEPPER SALAD

It is now possible to buy sweet peppers in a variety of colors, so include as many as you wish in this eye-catching salad.

3 red peppers
3 green peppers
3 yellow peppers
3 tbsps vegetable oil
9 tbsps sunflower oil
3 tbsps lemon juice
3 tbsps white wine vinegar
1 small clove garlic, minced
Pinch salt
Pinch cayenne pepper
Pinch sugar
3 hard-cooked eggs
⅓ cup black olives, pitted
3 tbsps finely chopped fresh coriander leaves, optional

Step 2 Put the cored pepper halves cut side down on a flat surface and gently press them with the palm of your hand to flatten them out.

Step 4 Cook the oiled peppers under the broiler until the skin begins to char and split.

1. Cut all the peppers in half and remove the seeds and cores.

2. With the palm of your hand lightly press the halved peppers down onto a flat surface, to flatten them out.

3. Brush the skin side of each pepper with a little of the vegetable oil and place under a preheated hot broiler.

4. Cook until the skins begin to char and split.

5. Remove the peppers from the broiler and wrap them in a clean dishtowel. Allow to stand for 10-15 minutes.

6. Put the sunflower oil, lemon juice, vinegar, garlic, salt, pepper and sugar into a small bowl and beat together well.

7. Shell the eggs and cut each one into four.

8. Unwrap the peppers and carefully peel away the burnt skin. Cut the pepper flesh into thick strips about 1-inch wide.

9. Arrange the pepper strips in a circle, alternating the colors all the way round.

10. Arrange the olives and quartered eggs in the center.

11. Sprinkle with the coriander leaves, and spoon over all the dressing.

12. Chill the salad for at least 1 hour before serving.

Cook's Notes

Time
Preparation takes 20 minutes, cooking takes about 5 minutes.

Serving Idea
Serve this salad with crusty French bread or rolls.

Cook's Tip
Peeled peppers will keep in a refrigerator for up to 5 days if they are covered with a little oil.

Fat Type
This recipe is high in polyunsaturated fats. The eggs contain saturated fats, but can be omitted if desired.

SERVES 4

CHEESY STUFFED TOMATOES

Although cheese should be avoided on a low fat diet, soft cheeses such as Brie and Camembert do have a lower fat content than Cheddar and in small amounts can provide welcome variety in a restricted diet.

4 beefsteak tomatoes
4 anchovy fillets
3 tsps capers, drained
2 green onions
1 cup Camembert or Brie cheese, rind removed
3 tsps caraway seeds
Salt and freshly ground black pepper
Lettuce to garnish

1. Cut a slice from the rounded end of each tomato and carefully scoop out the pulp and seeds. Strain out the seeds and reserve the pulp and juice for the filling.

Step 1 Strain the seeds out of the tomato pulp, keeping only the pulp and juice for use in the recipe.

2. Put the anchovies in a bowl and cover with a little milk. Allow to soak for 5 minutes to remove the saltiness.

3. Drain and rinse the anchovies, then pat them dry. Chop the anchovies finely.

4. Put the capers and green onions onto a board and chop them finely also.

5. Put the cheese into a bowl and mash it with a fork.

6. Stir in the capers, anchovies, onions, caraway seeds, tomato juice and pulp. Mix together thoroughly, then season with a little salt and pepper.

7. Carefully spoon the cheese filling into the hollowed out tomatoes and arrange them on a serving plate.

Step 7 Carefully pile the cheese filling back into the hollowed out tomatoes.

8. Replace the sliced tops and serve them well chilled on a bed of lettuce.

COOK'S NOTES

Time
Preparation takes 15 minutes, plus chilling time of at least 1 hour.

Preparation
Use a grapefruit knife or serrated teaspoon to remove the centers of the tomatoes.

Variation
Use cottage or curd cheese instead of the Camembert or Brie.

Serving Idea
Serve with a vinaigrette dressing and whole-wheat bread or rolls.

Fat Type
The cheese contains saturated fat, so should only be eaten in moderation.

SERVES 4

MEDITERRANEAN EGGPLANTS

These delicious stuffed eggplants can be served as an accompaniment to a main meal for four or as a lunch dish for two.

2 small eggplants
2 tbsps polyunsaturated margarine
1 small onion, finely chopped
1 clove garlic, minced
¼lb tomatoes
⅔ cup long grain rice, cooked
3 tsps fresh chopped marjoram
Pinch cinnamon
Salt and freshly ground black pepper

1. Preheat an oven to 350°F. Wrap the eggplants in aluminum foil and bake for 20 minutes to soften. Allow to cool.

2. Cut the eggplants in half, then using a serrated teaspoon or grapefruit knife, carefully scoop out the pulp leaving a ½-inch border to form a shell.

3. Melt the margarine in a frying pan and gently sauté the onion and garlic until they are just soft.

4. Chop the eggplant pulp roughly and stir into the pan along with the onions. Cover and cook for about 5 minutes.

5. Cut a small cross in the skins of the tomatoes and plunge them into boiling water for 30 seconds.

6. Remove the tomatoes from the water and carefully peel away the skin using a sharp knife.

7. Quarter the tomatoes and remove and discard the pips. Chop the tomato flesh roughly and stir into the cooked eggplant and onion mixture, along with the rice, marjoram and cinnamon. Season with salt and pepper.

8. Carefully pile the rice filling back into the eggplant shells and arrange them on an ovenproof dish or cookie sheet. Cover with aluminum foil.

9. Return to the oven and bake for 20 minutes. Serve hot, garnished with a little finely chopped parsley if desired.

Step 2 Carefully scoop the pulp out of each eggplant half with a serrated spoon or grapefruit knife, leaving a thin border on the inside to form a shell.

Step 7 Remove and discard the seeds from the peeled tomatoes.

Cook's Notes

 Time
Preparation takes 25 minutes, cooking takes about 40 minutes.

 Preparation
Take care not to split the eggplant shells when scooping out the pulp.

 Variation
½ cup mature Cheddar cheese can be added to the filling if desired or allowed!

 Fat Type
This recipe contains only polyunsaturated fats.

SERVES 4

CHICKEN WITH "BURNT" PEPPERS AND CORIANDER

"Burning" peppers is a technique for removing the skins which also imparts a delicious flavor to this favorite vegetable.

2 red peppers, halved and seeded
1 green pepper, halved and seeded
6 tbsps vegetable oil, for brushing
1½ tbsps olive oil
3 tsps paprika
Pinch ground cumin
Pinch cayenne pepper
2 cloves garlic, minced
1lb canned tomatoes, drained and chopped
4½ tbsps fresh chopped coriander
4½ tbsps fresh chopped parsley
Salt, for seasoning
4 large chicken breasts, boned
1 large onion, sliced
⅓ cup slivered almonds

1. Put the peppers, cut side down, on a flat surface and gently press them with the palm of your hand to flatten them out.

2. Brush the skin side with 3 tbsps of the vegetable oil and cook them under a hot broiler until the skin chars and splits.

3. Wrap the peppers in a clean towel for 10 minutes to cool.

4. Unwrap the peppers and carefully peel off the charred skin. Chop the pepper flesh into thin strips.

5. Heat the olive oil in a frying pan and gently fry the paprika, cumin, cayenne pepper and garlic for 2 minutes, stirring to prevent the garlic from browning.

6. Stir in the tomatoes, coriander, parsley and season with a little salt. Simmer for 15-20 minutes, or until thick. Set aside.

7. Heat the remaining vegetable oil in an ovenproof casserole dish, and sauté the chicken breasts, turning them frequently until they are golden brown on both sides.

8. Remove the chicken and set aside. Gently fry the onions in the oil for about 5 minutes, or until softened but not overcooked.

9. Return the chicken to the casserole with the onions and pour on about 1¼ cups of water. Bring to the boil.

10. Cover the casserole and simmer for about 30 minutes, turning the chicken occasionally to prevent it from burning.

11. Remove the chicken from the casserole and boil the remaining liquid rapidly to reduce to about ⅓ cup of stock.

12. Add the peppers and the tomato sauce to the chicken stock and stir well.

13. Return the chicken to the casserole, cover and simmer very gently for a further 30 minutes, or until the chicken is tender.

14. Arrange the chicken on a serving dish with a little of the sauce spooned over. Sprinkle with the almonds and serve any remaining sauce separately.

Cook's Notes

 Time
Preparation takes 30 minutes, cooking takes about 1 hour 30 minutes.

 Preparation
Take care not to cook this dish too rapidly or the peppers will disintegrate.

 Fat Type
The chicken contains saturated fats, but only in small quantities, the rest of the dish contains only polyunsaturated fat.

SERVES 4

HERRINGS WITH APPLES

The addition of fresh tasting apples beautifully complements the delicious and wholesome flavor of herring.

4 herrings, cleaned
2 large dessert apples
1 large onion
4 large potatoes, peeled and sliced
Salt and freshly ground black pepper
½ cup dry cider
1 cup dried breadcrumbs
¼ cup polyunsaturated margarine
1½ tbsps fresh chopped parsley

1. Cut the heads and tails from the herrings and split them open from the underside.

2. Put the herrings, belly side down, on a flat surface and carefully press along the back of each fish with the palm of your hand, pushing the backbone down towards the surface.

3. Turn the herrings over and with a sharp knife, carefully prise away the backbone, pulling out any loose bones as you go. Do not cut the fish into separate fillets. Wash and dry them well.

4. Peel, quarter, core and slice one of the apples. Peel and slice the onion thinly.

5. Lightly grease a shallow baking pan and layer with the potatoes, apple and onions, seasoning well with salt and pepper between layers.

6. Pour the cider over the potato layers and cover the dish with foil. Bake in a preheated oven 350°F for 40 minutes.

7. Remove the dish from the oven and arrange the herring fillets over the top.

8. Sprinkle the breadcrumbs over the herrings and dot

Step 2 Press down the backbone of the herrings with the palm of your hand, pushing the spine towards the work surface as you go.

Step 3 Carefully lift the backbone away from the fish with a sharp knife, pulling any loose bones out at the same time. Do not cut the fish into separate fillets.

with half of the margarine.

9. Increase the oven temperature to 400°F and return the dish to the oven for about 10–15 minutes, or until the herrings are cooked and brown.

10. Core the remaining apples and slice into rounds, leaving the peel on.

11. Melt the remaining margarine in a frying pan and gently fry the apple slices.

12. Remove the herrings from the oven and garnish with the fried apple slices and chopped parsley. Serve at once.

Cook's Notes

Time
Preparation takes 15-20 minutes, cooking takes about 50 minutes.

Variation
Use small mackerel instead of herrings in this recipe.

Serving Idea
Serve with a carrot, orange and watercress salad.

Fat Type
Fish contains mono-unsaturated fats which do not affect the cholesterol levels in the blood.

SERVES 6-8
SALMON TROUT WITH SPINACH AND WALNUT STUFFING

1 fresh whole salmon trout, weighing 2½lbs, cleaned
2lbs fresh spinach
1 small onion
¼ cup polyunsaturated margarine
½ cup walnuts, roughly chopped
2 cups fresh white breadcrumbs
1½ tbsps fresh chopped parsley
1½ tbsps fresh chopped thyme
Pinch grated nutmeg
Salt and freshly ground black pepper
Juice 2 lemons
Watercress sprigs and lemon slices, to garnish

1. Carefully cut the underside of the fish from the end of the slit made when the fish was cleaned, to the tip of the tail.

2. Place the fish, belly side down, on a flat work surface, spreading the cut underside out to balance the fish more easily.

3. Using the palm of your hand press down along the backbone of the fish, pushing the spine downwards towards the work surface.

4. Turn the fish over and using a sharp knife, carefully pull the backbone away from the fish, cutting it away with scissors at the base of the head and tail.

5. Remove the backbone completely and pull out any loose bones you may find with a pair of tweezers. Lay the boned fish in the center of a large square of lightly oiled aluminum foil and set aside.

6. Wash the spinach leaves well and tear off any coarse stalks. Put the spinach into a large saucepan and sprinkle with salt. Do not add any extra water. Cover and cook over a moderate heat for about 3 minutes.

7. Turn the spinach into a colander and drain well, pressing with the back of a wooden spoon to remove all the excess moisture.

8. Chop the cooked spinach very finely using a sharp knife.

9. Peel and chop the onion finely and fry gently in about 1 tbsp of the margarine until soft, but not colored.

10. Stir the cooked onion into the chopped spinach along with the walnuts, breadcrumbs, herbs, nutmeg, salt, pepper and half of the lemon juice. Mix well to blend evenly.

11. Use the spinach stuffing to fill the cavity inside the trout. Push the stuffing in firmly, re-shaping the fish as you do so. Allow a little of the stuffing to show between the cut edge of the fish.

12. Seal the foil over the top of the fish, but do not wrap it too tightly.

13. Place the fish in a roasting pan and bake in a preheated oven at 350°F for 35 minutes.

14. Carefully unwrap the fish and transfer it to a large serving dish.

15. Using a sharp knife, peel away the skin from all exposed sides of the fish. If possible remove some skin from the underside also.

16. Whilst the fish is still hot, dot with the remaining margarine, sprinkle with the remaining lemon juice. then serve garnished with the watercress and sliced lemon.

Cook's Notes

Time
Preparation takes 35-40 minutes, cooking takes about 40 minutes.

Cook's Tip
If you feel that you cannot bone the fish yourself, ask your fishmonger to do it for you, but explain that you wish the bone to be removed from the underside of the fish.

Fat Type
Fish contains mono-unsaturated fats and the remainder of fats used in this recipe are all polyunsaturated.

SERVES 4

SPANISH GUINEA FOWL

The olive oil in this recipe gives a wonderful flavor to the sauce without loading it with saturated fat.

4 small guinea fowl
Salt and freshly ground black pepper
Olive oil, to brush
4 small wedges of lime or lemon
4 bay leaves
3 tbsps olive oil
1 small onion, thinly sliced
1 clove garlic, peeled and minced
1lb tomatoes
⅔ cup red wine
⅔ cup chicken or vegetable stock
1½ tbsps tomato paste
1 green chilies, seeded and thinly sliced
1 small red pepper, seeded and cut into thin strips
1 small green pepper, seeded and cut into thin strips
3 tbsps chopped blanched almonds
1½ tbsps pine kernels
12 small black olives, pitted
1½ tbsps raisins

1. Rub the guinea fowl inside and out with salt and pepper. Brush the skins with olive oil and push a wedge of lemon or lime, and a bay leaf into the center of each one.

2. Roast the guinea fowl, uncovered, in a preheated oven 375°F for 45 minutes, or until just tender.

3. Heat the 3 tbsps olive oil in a large frying pan and gently cook the onion and the garlic until they are soft, but not colored.

4. Cut a slit into the skins of each tomato and plunge into boiling water for 30 seconds.

5. Using a sharp knife carefully peel away the skins from the blanched tomatoes.

6. Chop the tomatoes roughly. Remove and discard the seeds and cores.

7. Add the chopped tomatoes to the cooked onion and garlic, and fry gently for a further 2 minutes.

8. Add all the remaining ingredients and simmer for 10-15 minutes, or until the tomatoes have completely softened and the sauce has thickened slightly.

9. Arrange the guinea fowl on a serving dish and spoon a little of the sauce over each one.

10. Serve hot with the remaining sauce in a separate jug.

Step 3 Fry the onion and garlic gently in the olive oil until they are soft but not colored.

Step 5 Using a sharp knife carefully peel away the loosened skins from the blanched tomatoes.

Cook's Notes

Time
Preparation takes 15 minutes, cooking takes about 1 hour.

Serving Idea
Serve with rice and a mixed green salad.

Cook's Tip
If the guinea fowl start to get too brown during the cooking time, cover them with aluminum foil.

Fat Type
Chicken contains only small amounts of saturated fats, and the remaining ingredients in this recipe contain only unsaturated fats.

SERVES 4

SAFFRON CHICKEN

The delicate color and flavor of saffron enhances the taste of chicken and gives this dish a Mediterranean flavor.

2-3lb chicken
3 tbsps olive oil
Salt and freshly ground black pepper
1 small onion, peeled and finely chopped
1 clove garlic, minced
3 tsps paprika
8 tomatoes
1½ cups long grain white rice
2½ cups boiling water
Large pinch saffron strands or ¼ tsp ground saffron
1 cup frozen peas
3 tbsps chopped fresh parsley

1. Cut the chicken into 8 pieces with a sharp knife or cook's cleaver, cutting lengthwise down the breast bone and through the backbone, to halve it completely.

2. Cut the chicken halves in half again, slitting between the leg joint diagonally up and around the breast joint.

3. Finally cut each chicken quarter in half by cutting away the drumsticks from the leg thigh joint, and the wings from the breast joints.

4. Remove the skin from the chicken joints by pulling and cutting with a sharp knife.

5. Heat the oil in a large casserole dish or sauté pan, and fry the chicken, turning it frequently to brown evenly. Season with a little salt and pepper, then remove it from the pan and set aside.

6. Add the onions and garlic to the juices in the sauté pan and cook slowly until softened but not colored.

7. Add the paprika to the onions and fry quickly for about

Step 4 Remove the skin from the chicken joints by pulling and cutting with a sharp knife.

30 seconds to just burn.

8. Cut a small cross into the skins of the tomatoes and plunge them into boiling water.

9. Using a sharp knife peel away the loosened skin from each tomato.

10. Cut the tomatoes into quarters and remove the cores and seeds. Chop the tomato flesh finely and add this to the sauté pan with the paprika and the onions.

11. Cook for about 5-10 minutes to draw off the liquid from the tomatoes. The sauce mixture should be of a dropping consistency when this has been done.

12. Stir the rice, water and saffron into the tomato purée along with the browned chicken portions. Bring to the boil, reduce the heat to simmering, then cover the casserole tightly and cook for about 20 minutes.

13. Add the peas and the parsley to the casserole, stir well and continue cooking for a further 5-10 minutes, or until the rice is tender and all the liquids have been absorbed.

14. Serve very hot.

Cook's Notes

 Time
Preparation takes about 25 minutes, cooking takes 30-35 minutes.

! **Watchpoint**
Stir the casserole frequently after step 12 to prevent the rice from sticking.

 Fat Type
Chicken contains small amounts of saturated fat, but the remainder in this recipe is polyunsaturated.

SERVES 4

CHICKEN LIVER STIR-FRY

Chicken livers are very low in fat and high in flavor. They also require very little cooking so are perfect for stir-fry recipes.

1lb chicken livers
4½ tbsps sesame oil
⅓ cup split blanched almonds
1 clove garlic, peeled
⅓ cup snow peas, trimmed
8-10 Chinese cabbage leaves, shredded
3 tsps cornstarch
1½ tbsps cold water
3 tbsps soy sauce
⅔ cup chicken or vegetable stock

Step 1 Trim the chicken livers, cutting away any discolored areas or bits of fat or tubes using a sharp knife.

1. Trim the chicken livers, removing any discolored areas or fatty tubes.

2. Cut the chicken livers into even-sized pieces.

3. Heat a wok and pour in the oil. When the oil is hot, reduce the heat and stir-fry the almonds until they are pale golden brown. Remove the almonds, draining any oil back into the wok, and set them aside on kitchen towels.

Step 3 Stir-fry the almonds in the hot oil until they are a pale golden brown.

4. Add the garlic clove to the wok and cook for 1-2 minutes to flavor the oil only. Remove the clove of garlic and discard.

5. Stir the chicken livers into the flavored oil and cook for 2-3 minutes, stirring frequently to brown evenly. Remove the chicken livers from the wok and set them aside.

6. Add the snow peas to the hot oil and stir-fry for 1 minute. Then stir in the Chinese cabbage leaves and cook for 1 minute further. Remove the vegetables and set aside.

Step 8 Cook the sauce in the wok, stirring all the time until it has thickened and cleared.

7. Mix together the cornstarch and water, then blend in the soy sauce and stock.

8. Pour the cornstarch mixture into the wok and bring to the boil, stirring until the sauce has thickened and cleared.

9. Return all other ingredients to the wok and heat through for 1 minute. Serve immediately.

Cook's Notes

Time
Preparation takes 25 minutes, cooking takes 5-6 minutes.

Variation
Use finely sliced lamb or calves' liver in place of the chicken livers.

Serving Idea
Serve with fried rice or noodles.

Fat Type
Liver contains saturated fat, but in very small quantities.

SERVES 4-6

CHICKEN WITH LEMON JULIENNE

Lean chicken served with a tangy julienne of fresh vegetables makes a delicious main course – ideal for those on a low cholesterol diet.

1 x 3lb chicken
3 tbsps olive oil
3 tbsps polyunsaturated margarine
2 sticks celery
2 carrots
1 small onion, peeled and thinly sliced
1½ tbsps chopped fresh basil
1 bay leaf
Juice and grated rind of 2 small lemons
⅔ cup water
Salt and freshly ground black pepper
Pinch sugar, optional
Lemon slices for garnish

1. Cut the chicken into 8 pieces with a sharp knife or a cook's cleaver, cutting the chicken lengthwise down the breastbone and through the backbone to halve it completely.

2. Cut the chicken halves in half again, slitting between the leg joint diagonally up and around the breast joint.

3. Finally cut each chicken quarter in half by cutting away the drumsticks from the leg thigh joint, and the wings from the breast joints.

4. Remove the skin from the chicken joints by pulling and cutting with a sharp knife.

5. Heat the oil in a large sauté pan along with the margarine. Gently fry the chicken pieces, turning them frequently to brown evenly.

6. Remove the chicken pieces to a plate and set aside.

7. Using a sharp knife cut the celery into pieces 1½-inches long. Cut these pieces into long thin matchsticks lengthwise.

8. Cut the carrots into similar length pieces, then cut each piece in half lengthwise. Continue cutting each carrot half into the same sized pieces as the celery.

9. Stir the carrots and celery into the chicken juices, along with the onion. Cook over a gentle heat for about 3 minutes or until just beginning to soften but not brown.

10. Stir the basil, bay leaf, lemon juice and rind, the water, salt and pepper into the vegetables, mix well and cook for 2-3 minutes.

11. Return the chicken portions to the casserole and bring the mixture to the boil.

12. Cover the pan and reduce the heat. Allow the casserole to simmer for about 35-45 minutes, or until the chicken is tender and the juices will run clear when the meat is pierced with a sharp knife.

13. Remove the chicken and vegetables to a serving dish and discard the bay leaf.

14. Heat the sauce quickly to thicken if necessary. Adjust the flavor of the sauce with the sugar if desired.

15. Spoon the sauce over the chicken and garnish with the lemon slices.

Cook's Notes

 Time
Preparation takes 40 minutes, cooking will take about 55 minutes.

 Serving Idea
Serve with rice and a green salad.

 Watchpoint
Make sure that the chicken pieces are patted dry with paper towels before you fry them or the oil will spit.

 Fat Type
The chicken contains saturated fats in small amounts, the remainder is polyunsaturated fat.

SERVES 4

TROUT IN APSIC

This attractive main course is ideal for serving as a part of a summer's meal.

7½ cups water
Pinch salt
6 black peppercorns
2 bay leaves
2 sprigs fresh parsley
1 small onion, quartered
1¼ cups dry white wine
4 even-sized rainbow trout, cleaned and well washed
2 egg whites, softly beaten
3 tbsps powdered gelatin
Lemon slices, capers and sprigs of fresh dill, to garnish

1. Put the water, salt, peppercorns, bay leaves, parsley, onion and wine into a large saucepan or fish kettle. Bring to the boil and simmer for about 30 minutes.

2. Cool slightly, then lay the fish into the hot stock. Cover the pan and bring back to simmering point.

3. Cook the fish gently for 5 minutes, then remove from the heat.

4. Allow the fish to cool in the covered pan before removing and draining on paper towels.

5. Reserve the stock.

6. Using a sharp knife, carefully peel away the skin from the cooked fish.

7. Using a palette knife, lift the fillets from the top of each fish, taking great care that they do not break, and lay them on a large serving dish that has a slight well in the center.

8. Lift the backbone away from the lower fillets and discard.

9. Arrange the lower fish fillets on the serving dish along with the others.

10. Strain the reserved fish stock into a large saucepan through a nylon sieve to remove the spices, herbs and vegetables.

11. Add the egg whites to the fish stock and heat gently, whipping constantly with an eggbeater.

12. While you are whipping, the egg whites should form a thick frosty crust on top which removes all particles from the stock.

13. Bring the mixture to the boil then stop whipping and allow the egg whites and liquid to rise up the sides of the pan. Remove from the heat and allow to subside. Repeat this process twice more, then allow to settle completely.

14. Line a colander with several thicknesses of paper towels or cheesecloth and stand the colander over a large bowl. Pour the fish stock into the colander along with the egg whites and allow to drain slowly. Do not allow the egg whites to fall into the clarified liquid.

15. When the liquid has drained through, remove about ½ cup and heat it gently. Sprinkle over the gelatin and allow to stand until the gelatin has dissolved completely.

16. Mix the gelatin mixture into the remaining stock and allow to cool in a refrigerator until just beginning to set.

17. Decorate the trout and the base of the dish with the lemon slices, capers and dill.

18. When the aspic has become syrupy and slightly thickened, spoon it carefully over the fish fillets for decoration.

19. Place the serving plate into a refrigerator and chill until set (about 1-2 hours).

Cook's Notes

Time
Preparation takes 45 minutes to 1 hour. Total cooking time is about 50 minutes plus at least 1 hour to chill the dish.

Watchpoint
Do not stir or whip the aspic or bubbles will form and these will spoil the appearance. For speed you can use powdered aspic, available from most delicatessens.

Fat Type
Fish contains mono-unsaturated fats, and there are no other fats in this recipe.

SERVES 6
TURKEY KEBABS

*For this low fat dish, use the ready-prepared turkey joints which are now easily
available from supermarkets or butchers.*

3lbs lean turkey meat
3 tsps fresh chopped sage
1 sprig rosemary, chopped
Juice 1 lemon
3 tbsps olive oil
Salt and freshly ground black pepper
¼lb lean back bacon, rind removed
Whole sage leaves

1. Remove any bone from the turkey and cut the meat into even-sized cubes.

2. Put the chopped sage, rosemary, lemon juice, oil, salt and pepper into a large bowl and stir in the turkey meat, mixing well to coat evenly. Cover and leave in the refrigerator overnight.

3. Cut the bacon strips into half lengthwise and then again crosswise.

4. Wrap these pieces around as many of the cubes of

marinated turkey meat as possible.

5. Thread the turkey and bacon rolls alternately with the sage leaves and any unwrapped turkey cubes onto kebab skewers.

6. Heat the broiler to moderate, and cook the kebabs under the heat for 30 minutes, turning frequently and basting with the marinade whilst cooking. Serve immediately.

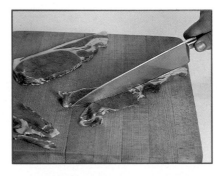

Step 3 Cut the bacon slices in half lengthwise and then again crosswise.

Step 2 Stir the cubed turkey pieces into the marinade, mixing well to coat evenly.

Step 4 Carefully roll each piece of marinated turkey in a strip of bacon.

Cook's Notes

 Time
Preparation takes 20 minutes, plus overnight soaking.
Cooking takes about 30 minutes.

 Variation
Use chicken if preferred.

 Serving Idea
Serve with pitta bread and salad, or on a bed of rice.

 Fat Type
Both chicken and turkey contain low amounts of saturated fat. The bacon contains saturated fat, but this will be reduced whilst broiling.

SERVES 6

GREEN GRAPE SHORTCAKE

Plenty of fiber in the diet will help to reduce the amount of cholesterol found in the blood, and the whole-wheat flour and grape skins in this recipe are a good source of fiber.

¼ cup polyunsaturated margarine
2 tbsps soft brown sugar
½ cup whole-wheat flour
¼ cup ground almonds
½lb green grapes, halved and pitted
2½ cups water
Thinly pared rind of 2 lemons
1½ tbsps honey
1 tbsp powdered gelatin
Few drops yellow food coloring, optional

1. Put the margarine, sugar, flour and almonds into a large bowl.

2. Work the margarine into the dry ingredients using your fingertips, and pressing the mixture together gently to form a soft dough.

3. Knead the dough lightly until it is smooth.

4. Line the base of a 8-inch loose-bottomed cake pan with silicone paper. Press the shortcake dough evenly over the base of the lined pan, making sure that it is pushed well into the sides.

5. Bake in a preheated oven 375°F for 15 minutes, or until the shortcake is firm and golden brown. Remove from the oven and allow to cool in the pan.

6. Lightly oil the inside of the cake pan above the shortcake with a little vegetable oil.

7. Arrange the grape halves on top of the shortcake.

8. Put the pint of water and lemon rind into a small pan and bring to the boil. Allow to simmer for 5 minutes, then remove the pan from the heat and allow the liquid to cool completely.

9. Strain the lemon liquid through a nylon sieve to remove the rinds. Measure off 2 cups of the strained liquid and stir in the honey.

10. Put the remaining lemon liquid into a small saucepan and heat gently until it is very hot, but not boiling.

11. Sprinkle over the gelatin and allow to stand until it has completely dissolved.

Step 7 Arrange the grape halves over the cooked shortcake whilst it is still in the pan.

12. At this stage the food coloring can be added to the liquid if desired.

13. Stir the gelatin mixture into the lemon and honey mixture and stand in a cool place until it is beginning to set.

14. Spoon the partially set jelly carefully over the grapes making sure that they remain evenly spread.

15. Stand the shortcake in a refrigerator until the jelly has set completely. Serve in wedges.

Cook's Notes

 Time
Preparation takes 45 minutes, plus cooling and chilling.
Cooking takes about 20 minutes.

 Preparation
It is important never to boil gelatin or it will not dissolve completely.

 Fat Type
The fat in this recipe is polyunsaturated.

SERVES 4

SPICED ORANGES WITH HONEY AND MINT

An unusual combination of flavors blend to create this light and very refreshing dessert.

1¼ cups clear honey
1½ cups water
2 large sprigs of fresh mint
12 whole cloves
4 large oranges
4 small sprigs of mint, to garnish

1. Put the honey and the water into a heavy-based saucepan. Add the mint and cloves, and slowly bring to the boil.

2. Stir the mixture to dissolve the honey and boil rapidly for 5 minutes, or until the liquid is very syrupy.

3. Cool the mixture completely, then strain the syrup through a nylon sieve into a jug or bowl to remove the sprigs of mint and cloves.

4. Using a potato peeler, carefully pare the rind very thinly from one orange.

5. Cut the pared orange rind into very fine shreds with a sharp knife.

6. Put the shreds of orange peel into a small bowl and cover with boiling water. Allow to stand until cold then drain completely, reserving only the strips of peel.

7. Stir the strips of peel into the honey syrup and chill well.

8. Peel the oranges completely, removing all the skin and especially the white pith.

Step 3 Strain the syrup through a nylon sieve into a jug or bowl to remove the sprigs of mint and cloves.

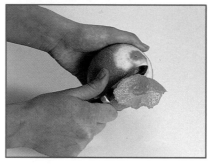

Step 4 Carefully pare the rind from one of the oranges, using a potato peeler and making sure that no white pith comes away with the rind.

9. Slice the oranges into thin rounds using a sharp knife. Arrange the orange rounds onto four individual serving plates.

10. Pour the chilled syrup over the oranges on the plates and garnish with the small sprigs of mint just before serving.

COOK'S NOTES

Time
Preparation takes 20 minutes, cooking takes about 5 minutes.

Fat Type
There is no fat in this recipe.

Preparation
It is important that all the white pith is removed from the oranges, otherwise this will give a bitter flavor to the dessert.

Variation
Use ruby grapefruits in place of the oranges in this recipe. Allow half a grapefruit per person, and cut it into segments rather than slices to serve.

SERVES 4-6

BRANDY SORBET WITH APPLES AND GOLDEN RAISINS

Sorbets make an ideal dessert for anyone on a low fat diet. Try this unusual combination for a real change of flavors.

2½ cups apple juice
¼ cup superfine sugar
½ cup of dried apple flakes
⅔ cup golden raisins
⅔ cup brandy
Few drops green food coloring, optional
1 egg white

1. Put the apple juice in a heavy-based saucepan along with the sugar. Heat gently, stirring until the sugar has dissolved. Bring the apple juice to the boil and boil quickly for 5 minutes. Remove from the heat and cool completely.

2. Put the apple flakes into a bowl along with the golden raisins and brandy. Add enough of the apple syrup to cover the mixture, then allow to soak for 4 hours.

3. Mix the apple flakes, golden raisins and brandy together to form a pulp, adding the green coloring at this stage if required.

4. Whip the apple pulp into the remaining syrup, mixing thoroughly to blend evenly.

5. Pour the apple mixture into a shallow container and freeze for 2 hours or until just beginning to set.

6. Break up the partially frozen ice using a fork or electric whisk, then return to the freezer tray and continue to freeze for another hour.

7. Break up the ice crystals again, but this time mash thoroughly until they form a thick slush.

8. Whip the egg white until it is stiff, then quickly fold into the ice slush. Return to the freezer tray and freeze until completely solid.

9. Allow the ice to soften for 15 minutes before spooning into individual glass dishes.

Step 3 Beat the apple and golden raisin mixture with a fork until it becomes a thick purée.

Step 8 Fold the whipped egg whites carefully into the slushy ice before freezing completely.

Cook's Notes

 Time
Preparation takes 10 minutes, plus the soaking and freezing time.

Cook's Tip
Use 1 cup of apple purée in place of the apple flakes and reduce the amount of apple juice used to 2 cups.

 Variation
Omit the brandy from this recipe and replace with more apple juice.

 Fat Type
There is no fat of any kind in this recipe.

SERVES 6

PLUM AND HONEY COBBLER

A cobbler is a traditional English dessert, so called because of the scones which decorate the top are reminiscent of the cobbles found on old roads.

2lbs ripe plums, halved and pitted
6-9 tbsps clear honey
2 cups whole-wheat all-purpose flour
3 tbsps superfine sugar
¼ cup polyunsaturated margarine
7-9 tbsps skim milk
1 egg, beaten

1. Put the plums into an ovenproof dish along with the honey. Cover with a sheet of foil and cook in a preheated oven 400°F for 20 minutes.

2. After this time the plums should be soft and a certain amount of juice should have formed in the dish. Remove from the oven and cool completely.

3. Put the flour and the sugar into a large bowl and using your fingers, rub in the margarine until the mixture resembles fine breadcrumbs.

4. Using a round bladed knife, stir in the milk and eggs, so that the mixture forms a soft dough.

5. Turn the dough out onto a lightly floured work surface and knead it until it is smooth.

6. Roll the dough out until it is about ½-inch thick.

7. Cut the dough into rounds using a 2-inch cutter to form the cobbles.

8. Carefully arrange the scone cobbles in a circle around

Step 4 Mix the milk and egg into the flour using a round bladed knife, and pressing all ingredients together to form a soft dough.

Step 8 Arrange a circle of scone cobbles around the top edge of the dish, overlapping each one slightly.

the top edge of the dish of plums, overlapping each scone slightly.

9. Brush the top of each scone with a little milk and sprinkle with a little extra sugar. Return the plum cobbler to the oven, set at the same temperature as before, and cook until the scones are firm, risen and well browned.

10. Serve hot.

Cook's Notes

Time
Preparation takes 30 minutes, cooking takes 45 minutes.

Variation
Use any variation of fresh fruit in place of the plums.

Serving Idea
This dessert is delicious hot with a scoop of vanilla ice cream, but do check the fat content of the ice cream first.

Fat Type
The fats used in recipe are polyunsaturated.

SERVES 6

PEARS IN RED WINE

A delicious way of serving whole fresh pears, this dessert looks especially impressive served in glass dishes.

2½ cups dry red wine
Juice of half a lemon
1 strip lemon peel
1¼ cups sugar
1 small piece cinnamon stick
6 pears, ripe but firm
1½ tbsps slivered almonds

1. Put the wine, lemon juice, peel, sugar and cinnamon into a large deep saucepan and bring to the boil, stirring until the sugar dissolves.

2. Allow to boil rapidly for 1 minute.

3. Carefully peel the pears lengthwise and remove the small eye from the base of each pear. Leave any stalk which may be at the top intact.

4. Place the peeled pears upright in the boiled wine mixture.

5. Return the pan to the heat, bring to the boil, then simmer very gently for 20 minutes, or until the pears are soft but not mushy. Allow the pears to cool in the syrup until lukewarm, then remove and arrange in a serving dish.

6. Strain the syrup through a nylon sieve to remove the lemon peel and spices.

7. Return the syrup to the saucepan and boil rapidly until it becomes thicker and syrupy.

8. Cool the syrup completely before spooning it carefully over the pears in the serving dish.

9. Before serving, sprinkle with the slivered almonds.

Step 3 Peel the pears lengthwise and carefully remove the eye from the base of each one.

Step 4 Stand the pears in the saucepan of wine syrup; if it is possible to stand them upright and still have them covered by the sauce, then do so.

Step 5 The pears are cooked when they are soft, but not mushy and they are an even red color all over.

Cook's Notes

Time
Preparation takes 25 minutes, cooking takes 30 minutes.

Preparation
If the syrup does not completely cover the pears in the saucepan, allow them to cook on their side, but make sure they are turned frequently and basted, to ensure an even color.

Variation
Use white wine in place of the red wine in this recipe.

Fat Type
There is no fat in this recipe.

SERVES 6

CARIBBEAN FRUIT SALAD

This fruit salad is made from a refreshing mixture of tropical fruits, all of which are now easily available in most supermarkets.

½ cantaloup or honeydew melon, seeds removed
½ small pineapple
¼lb fresh strawberries
1 mango
½lb watermelon
¼lb guava
2 oranges
½ cup superfine sugar
⅔ cup white wine
Grated rind and juice of 1 lemon

---

1. Using a melon baller or teaspoon, scoop out rounds of flesh from the cantaloup or honeydew melon.

2. Cut the piece of pineapple in half lengthwise and carefully peel away the outer skin.

3. Remove any eyes left in the outside edge of the pineapple using a potato peeler.

4. Cut away the core from the pineapple with a serrated knife and slice the flesh thinly. Put the slices of pineapple into a large bowl along with the melon rounds.

5. Hull the strawberries and halve them. Add them to the bowl with the pineapple and melon.

6. Peel the mango, and carefully cut the flesh away from the long stone in the center of the fruit. Slice the flesh lengthwise, and stir it into the bowl of fruit.

7. Peel the watermelon and guavas, then cube the flesh. Stir these into the bowl of fruit.

8. Remove the rind from the oranges using a serrated knife. Take care to remove all the white pith, or this will flavor the fruit salad.

9. Cut the orange into segments, carefully removing the inner membrane from the segments as you slice.

10. Put the sugar, wine, lemon juice and rind into a small saucepan and warm through gently, stirring all the time until the sugar has dissolved. Do not boil, then set aside to cool.

11. Put the syrup into the bowl along with the fruit and mix thoroughly. Chill the fruit salad completely before serving.

Step 3 Remove any eyes which remain in the pineapple flesh with the pointed end of a potato peeler.

Step 6 Carefully cut the flesh away from the long inner stone of the mango, before slicing it lengthwise.

Cook's Notes

 Time
Preparation takes 45 minutes, cooking takes about 3 minutes.

 Fat Type
There are no fats at all in this recipe.

 Preparation
It is unnecessary to remove the pips from the watermelon unless you particularly dislike them.

 Watchpoint
Do not boil the syrup otherwise the flavor of the wine will be reduced.

Index

COMPILED BY PATRICIA PAYNE
EDITED BY JILLIAN STEWART
PHOTOGRAPHY BY PETER BARRY
RECIPES STYLED BY HELEN BURDETT
DESIGNED BY SALLY STRUGNELL
COVER DESIGN BY MARILYN O'NEONS